D0994996

So You Think You Know About...
STEGOSAURUS?

BEN GARROD

So You Think You Know About...
STEGOSAURUS?

ZEPHYR

First published in the UK in 2018 by Zephyr,
an imprint of Head of Zeus, Ltd

9 8 7 6 5 4 3 2 1

A CIP catalogue record for this book is available from the British Library.

ISBN (HB): 9781786697929
ISBN (E): 9781786697912

Designed by Sue Michniewicz

Printed and bound in Germany by CPI Books GmbH

Head of Zeus Ltd
First Floor East
5–8 Hardwick Street
London EC1R 4RG

WWW.HEADOFZEUS.COM

For geeky scientists
who are super-heroes too

CONTENTS

I was born loving animals. I used to watch birds and squirrels and frogs in our garden and on the cliffs above the sea. When I was ten years old, I decided I would go to Africa, live with wild animals and write books about them. Everyone laughed – Africa was far away – and I was just a girl. Back then (1944), girls didn't get to do things like that. But my mother said, 'If you really want this you must work hard, take advantage of opportunities, and *never give up.'* That is the message I have for you.

My dream came true when I met Dr Louis Leakey and was able to study chimpanzees in Gombe National Park, Tanzania. Chimpanzees helped me prove to science that like humans, animals have personalities, minds and emotions. Eventually I built a research station and my students are *still* learning new things about the Gombe chimpanzees. Just as scientists are always learning about new species of dinosaur.

INTRODUCTION

by **Jane Goodall**, PhD, DBE
Founder - the Jane Goodall Institute
& UN Messenger of Peace

I have known Dr Ben for years and he and I both encourage you to follow *your* dreams. Maybe you don't plan to be a scientist, but even so you need to learn about the work scientists do, for it helps us understand so much about the wonderful world we live in – about evolution and the incredible variety of species. And there are many more species not yet discovered. Maybe you will discover one of them! Maybe it will be named after you!

Whatever you decide to do, I hope you'll always be curious about our magical world and inspired by the people who spend their lives uncovering her secrets and sharing them. And, above all, that you will join Dr Ben and me in our efforts to conserve life on planet Earth.

Hey Guys

Okay, I have a confession. I was wrong. I don't often admit it, but I used to think that to be a scientist you had to have been to school and university, and then work in a laboratory or a rainforest, like a 'real' scientist. But then something weird happened to me. The more qualified I became (I've been to three universities now), and the more I worked in steamy rainforests, hot deserts, tropical islands and coral reefs, the more I realised that **any of us can be a scientist at any age**. If you're interested in and passionate about science, then you are a scientist.

Science is for every single one of us. It surrounds us in every part of our lives. **All you need to be a scientist is to find a way to 'take part'**. Do you count the number of birds in your garden and feed those results into national surveys? Do you collect fossils and record the details of where and when you found them? Do you have a wormery and watch how they break down leaf litter and household waste into soil? Do you help collect plastic litter from a beach nearby to save seabirds? All of these things are done by scientists . . . you don't need a white lab coat, test tubes and a brain the size of a planet to make you a scientist. Maybe you blog about science, or take photographs, or maybe you just do stuff by yourself and don't tell anyone. Doing anything like this means you are part of the 'scientist club', a really cool and really geeky club. **A club that contains astronauts and engineers, shark biologists and mathematicians, tree experts and, of course, palaeontologists.**

My parents were not scientists and there were none in my family, but when I was little I was lucky to meet a scientist called Percy who didn't treat me like I was 'just a kid'. It helped me feel that **I could talk about science and be part of this cool worldwide web of amazing people.** When I was a lot older, I met another great scientist, Dr Jane Goodall, and I chatted to her. She had famously been working with wild chimpanzees in Africa for nearly 50 years but there she was, talking to me. I was very lucky because I managed to get a job working for Jane and ended up living in a jungle in a mud hut, following chimpanzees every day. When I think about it now, I know I've got the best job in the world because I love the work I do and because, ever since I was young, I thought of myself as a scientist.

If you think you might be a young scientist, then remember that you are already part of this very big club, where you can have a conversation with anyone around the world about the science you love. I guarantee that wherever you go, you'll always find another scientist happy to talk about their work and how you can get more involved in your own area of science. Okay, there could be a couple of grumpy scientists who still think that science is for 'real' scientists, but most of us would love to encourage you.

Being a scientist is great fun but it is not always easy, especially when you're young. It might not seem as cool as being sporty or fashionable but that's okay. No one is saying you can't be sporty and a scientist, no one is saying you have to be into fashion and science. Just be yourself.

There are over seven billion people on planet Earth (that's 7, 000 000 000) and each of us is different. Imagine how boring it would be if we all liked the same things. **Be proud of who you are** and what you love doing and remember, with so many other young scientists out there, you will always have someone who likes the same sort of things you do. Start to think about what it means to be a young scientist and imagine the interesting conversations you might have, the amazing scientists you might meet and the incredible things that you will do.

Let's get geeky!

Ben

CHAPTER 1

Dinosaur Definitions

WHAT *IS* A DINOSAUR?

If you look in my other *So You Think You Know About . . . Dinosaurs?* books, you'll see that there are lots of ways scientists identify whether fossilised bones are from a dinosaur or not. Dinosaurs have clues on their bones, all the way from the tip of their skull to their legs and claws and everything in between. One of the most important areas is the skull. It can quickly tell us whether we are looking at a dinosaur, a close relative of a dinosaur or something totally different.

Dinosaurs are diapsids. This means they have two special holes behind each eye, towards the back of the skull. If you were wondering, we (as part of the mammal group) belong to the synapsids, and have one hole behind each eye.

Diapsid

Synapsid

Which of these skulls is from an early mammal and which is from a dinosaur?

There are lots of examples of extinct animals that may look like dinosaurs but are very different and in some cases more related to us than they were to the dinosaurs. One of the most common mistaken identities happens with the 'flying dinosaurs', the pterosaurs. Well, they are not dinosaurs and never were. All the pterosaurs, such as the famous *Pterodactylus* (*terra dack-tee luss*) and *Quetzalcoatlus* (*kwet-zal coat-luss*) were flying reptiles, not dinosaurs.

It's also easy to look at the prehistoric marine predators like mosasaurs (*moze a-saws*), pliosaurs (*pli o-saws*) and ichthyosaurs (*ick-thee o-saws*) and think, 'hey look, dinosaurs', but guess what . . . none of them were dinosaurs either. They

were prehistoric marine reptiles. There were even some weird animals such as the bizarre-looking *Shringasaurus indicus* (*Shh ring-ga saw-us indi-kus*), which was only discovered and described in 2017. It was 3–4m long and found in India, and many scientists commented on just how odd it looked. Whereas pterosaurs and marine predators like ichthyosaurs were alive at the time of the dinosaurs, *Shringasaurus* lived over 240 million years ago, around the same time as the very, very first dinosaurs were evolving. Like the others, *Shringasaurus* was not a dinosaur either, but belonged to a very old group of animals called the archosauromorphs (*ar-ko saw-a morffs*). The archosauromorphs were early reptiles, which went on to evolve into dinosaurs, pterosaurs, crocodiles and birds.

Shringasaurus

One of my favourite animals of all time, and one of the most famous examples of the 'Is it a dinosaur?' puzzle, is the *Dimetrodon* (*dim-et-ro don*) . . . a huge, four-legged monstrous animal that lived over 270 million years ago during the Permian in Germany and what is now the USA. Some species within the group were over

4.5m in length and had large spines coming off the back of the vertebrae, making a tall sail along the back.

Dimetrodon

Dimetrodon looked like a reptile and behaved like one, but was not a reptile. It also looked like a dinosaur and behaved like one, but was not a dinosaur. Many people think it was a dinosaur but it actually went extinct 40 million years before the first dinosaurs appeared and weirdly, it was more closely related to mammals than it was to modern reptiles.

Although we mammals did not evolve directly from *Dimetrodon*, we say it belongs to a group called the mammal-like reptiles (but remember, they are not mammals or reptiles or dinosaurs). The proper name is 'non-mammalian synapsids'. And you can remember what a synapsid is, right? How many holes do they have in the side of their skull? It basically means it was one of the animal groups with one hole behind each eye but not a mammal, which also has one hole behind each eye. So although it looked as though it could fit in with *Tyrannosaurus rex* and *Triceratops*, it is more closely related to you than it was to a *T. rex.* Sounds absolutely bonkers, doesn't it, but this is what science is sometimes . . . the more you study something and understand it, the weirder it becomes. Cool, hey!

DEFINITELY DINOSAURS

When we look at the puzzles caused by animals such as the ichthyosaurs and pterosaurs, and by *Shringasaurus* and *Dimetrodon*, it may seem confusing. But these examples of animals that looked like dinosaurs, but were in fact something very different, help to show us not only how hard palaeontology can be, but also how important it is to be able to correctly identify stuff in science. Whether you're working with jellyfish or trees or, of course, dinosaurs, it is vital to know how to correctly identify what you're working with.

Here is a checklist of all the things palaeontologists look for when identifying dinosaurs. See how many you can see next time you're in your local museum.

 **1. Dinosaurs have two holes behind each eye towards the back of the skull.** This means they are diapsids.

2. Dinosaurs all had straight legs. Next time you see a crocodile when you're out for a walk, have a look at its legs (just don't get too close). Rather than legs that stand straight like ours, their legs bend out in the middle somewhere. All reptiles with legs, such as crocs and their relatives and many lizards, have legs that look the same – they come out from the body to the side and then go down.

CROCODILE

DINOSAUR

All dinosaurs (whether with four legs or two) walked with their legs held in a straight line beneath their body. This meant dinosaurs could breathe easily as they walked or ran – great for chasing other dinosaurs, or running away from them. It also allowed them to become much bigger than if they had legs with a bend in the middle.

3. Dinosaurs had short arms. We all know that *Tyrannosaurus rex* and its relatives had teeny arms, but almost every dinosaur had forelimbs slightly shorter than you might expect. Have a look at your arms – the upper arm bone (humerus) is only a little longer than the two lower arm bones (radius and ulna). In dinosaurs, the radius is nearly always at least 20 per cent shorter than the humerus.

HUMAN   **DINOSAUR**

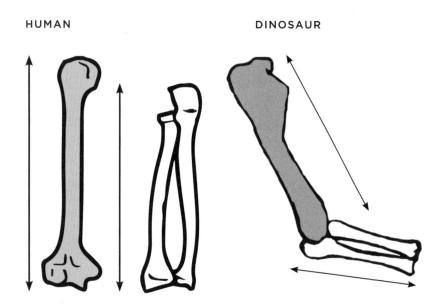

DINO CHECKLIST

Between the two holes behind the eye, there is a dimple (called a **fossa**) in the bone.

Most of the neck bones (**vertebrae**) have extra bits of bone that look like a little diagonally backwards-facing wing on each side. These are called '**epipophyses**' (*eppi-pofe ee-sees*).

There is a ridge along the edge of the **humerus** for big muscles to attach to. In dinosaurs, this ridge is more than 30 per cent of the way along the bone.

The ridge (called the **fourth trochanter**) on the **femur** (thigh bone), which the leg muscles attach to, is strong and looks 'sharp'.

The bones at the back of the **skull** do not meet in the middle.

The ridge on the **tibia** (shin bone) curves to the front and outwards.

At the place where the **fibula** (one of the lower leg bones) joins the ankle, there's a dip on the ankle bone.

How many dinosaurs were there? Sounds like an easy question, but the truth is that we don't really know. Some scientists say there were around 800, while others believe there may have been more than 1,000 species. The reason we don't know is because some of these species are named from just a few pieces of small broken fossils and there's not enough evidence to be certain that the fossils are from a new species. Sometimes scientists argue about whether a new discovery is from a new species or not.

Lots of people ask me how many more dinosaurs are yet to be discovered. We will never know how many more are still out there (unless we find them all), but remember – there are about 10,000 species of birds alive today so there are probably loads more dinosaurs waiting to be discovered.

CHAPTER 2

Dinosaur Detectives

Stegosaurus

Think of a vegetarian celebrity . . . how many can you think of? Okay, now try it again but this time you can count dinosaur 'celebrities' . . . that list becomes a lot easier, doesn't it? Things like *Argentinosaurus, Ankylosaurus* and *Triceratops* definitely appear on that list. So does the best well-known plant-muncher in (pre)history, *Stegosaurus*. Most people can recognise *Stegosaurus*, it's one of the most famous and most easily identifiable species of dinosaur ever. When trying to identify a *Stegosaurus*, the solid four-legged body and small head are useful clues, but the big giveaways are the rows of plates along the back and the huge spikes at the end of the tail. They make *Stegosaurus* and its closest relatives hard to mistake. *Stegosaurus* may not have a reputation for being the coolest dinosaur ever, but this heavily armoured herbivore was in fact full of secrets and surprises.

The first *Stegosaurus* fossils were found in 1876 in Colorado, USA, by a man called Mr Felch. The bones were scientifically described and a year later, they were officially named by the famous palaeontologist Othaniel Marsh. Along with his big team of fossil hunters, Marsh identified hundreds of new species of fossil animals, including lots of dinosaurs, such as *Triceratops*, *Apatosaurus* and *Allosaurus* and of course *Stegosaurus*. Imagine how you would feel if you and your mates discovered and named all these cool dino species. *Stegosaurus* lived during the Late Jurassic, between 150.8 million and 155.7 million years ago and was mostly found across western North America. It was a large, 3m long 2 tonne plant-eating dinosaur, but could reach a maximum size of 9m and weigh a massive 7 tonnes.

For many types of dinosaurs, we often have the puzzle of working out exactly how many species there were. For example, there was probably only one species of *Tyrannosaurus*, and scientists are sure there were two species of *Diplodocus*, but *Stegosaurus* has caused a lot of debate over the years. Some scientists have said there may have been as many as ten species of *Stegosaurus* but right now, most agree that there were definitely at least two species, *Stegosaurus stenops* and *Stegosaurus ungulatus*. There *may* be a third, *Stegosaurus sulcatus*, but there's not as much fossil evidence for it yet and, the truth is, we don't know if it was, or wasn't, different enough to be a separate species. This might change in the future but for now, two is enough.

FAMILY TREE

Stegosaurus was a genus of ornithischian dinosaur
(which included the horned dinosaurs like *Triceratops*
and others such as *Iguanodon* and its relatives and
Pachycephalosaurus). They were armoured dinosaurs,

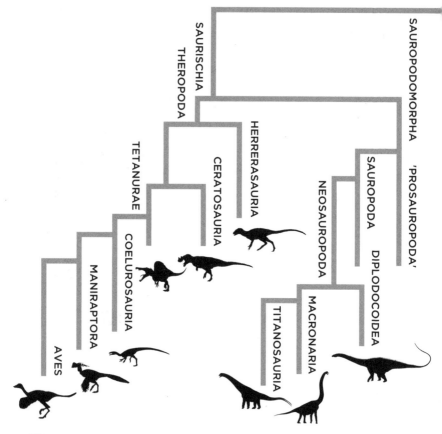

belonging to a group called Thyreophora (*thi-ree-o for-a*). This group also includes the ankylosaurs. Stegosaurid dinosaurs were found across North America, Africa and Asia.

DINOSAURIA

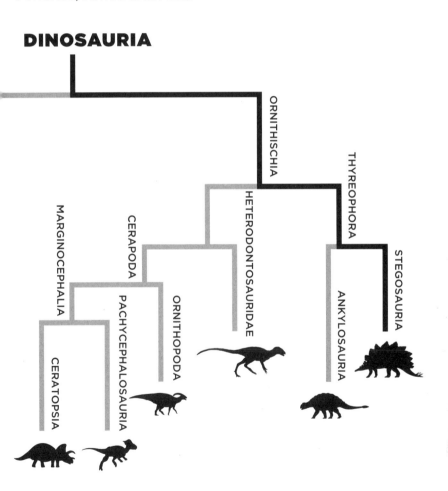

Stegosauridae

There were quite a few stegosaurid dinosaurs. They were all herbivores and they walked on four short legs, had a small head and large hips. The main differences between species were mainly in the shape, size and arrangement of spikes and plates that ran down the body. Some species had one row, others had two.

Stegosaurus was part of the Stegosauridae, which was in a bigger group called Stegosauria. Species such as *Kentrosaurus* and *Wuerhosaurus* were close relatives and were part of the same group.

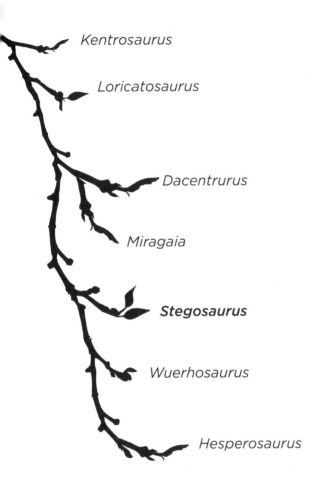

Kentrosaurus

Loricatosaurus

Dacentrurus

Miragaia

Stegosaurus

Wuerhosaurus

Hesperosaurus

Always remember that working with dinosaurs and other extinct species is like doing a jigsaw with most of the pieces missing. Until you find all the bones, you can never be 100 per cent certain about things and *Stegosaurus* has caused arguments between palaeontologists. Some have said there were two species, others say there were as many as ten.

One trouble-maker was from Madagascar. Scientists found some teeth in 1926 and thought they were from a new species. Then they were thought to be from a theropod or a crocodile, but now we think they probably belong to an ankylosaur. There have been lots of examples with *Stegosaurus* mistaken identity over the years.

Ankylosaur

STEGOSAURUS RELATIVES

Stegosaurus ungulatus (*Steggo saw-rus ung-yew lart-eez*) 'roof lizard with hooves'

2 m

9 m

This was the other species of *Stegosaurus* (that we can be certain of). It was also the biggest, reaching 9m in length. The two *Stegosaurus* species looked similar but there are differences. Imagine them standing side by side. This one had longer back legs than *Stegosaurus stenops* and its femurs and pelvis were longer. Its plates were more pointed and smaller, but still with wide bases and narrow tips. It had a few pairs of small flat bony plates above the tail spikes. Many old drawings of this species show eight tail spikes, not the four scientists now believe they had.

Wuerhosaurus (*Wear-oh saw-rus*) 'lizard from Wuerho'

2 m

7 m

Wuerhosaurus was a genus of stegosaurid from the Early Cretaceous and was found in Mongolia and China. Because *Wuerhosaurus* lived in the Late Jurassic, it was one of the very last of the stegosaur dinosaurs to be alive. Only a small section of the skeleton has been found, so although scientists cannot be sure, they think it was around 7m long and weighed a little over 4 tonnes. Some of the first scientists to study this animal thought the plates were flatter and much rounder than those of its relatives, but we now think perhaps they were broken. The body of *Wuerhosaurus* was closer to the ground than most other stegosaurid dinosaurs, allowing it to feed on low-growing plants.

Gigantspinosaurus (*Ji-gant spy-no saw-rus*)
'giant-spined lizard'

This weird-looking stegosaurid lived in the Late Jurassic
and was found across the Sichuan area of China. It
was a medium-sized stegosaur dinosaur, just over
4m long and weighed a little more than half a tonne.
Gigantspinosaurus had small, triangular plates behind
its head and along its neck and had a head larger than
many of its relatives. The hip bones were very big and
solid and some of the vertebrae in the pelvis and tail
were fused together in a solid block, meaning there
was a lot of power in its back end. Its most impressive
features were the two massive shoulder spines.
Although we are not fully sure if they were using them
for display or defence (or both), they were very cool,
impressive-looking dinosaurs.

Kentrosaurus (*Kent-ro saw-rus*) 'prickle lizard'

2m

4.5m

This stegosaurid lived in what is now Tanzania, during the Late Jurassic. We used to think this was an early member of the stegosaur dinosaur group but we now know that it was quite closely related to *Stegosaurus*. *Kentrosaurus* was about 4.5m in length and weighed a little over one tonne.

Unlike many of the other stegosaurids, especially those from North America, it had a double row of plates running all the way down from its head along its back. These merged into spikes about halfway down its back, and continued to the tail, where the spikes were the longest. It also had a pair of long sharp spines on the shoulders, for defence or display.

The name *Stegosaurus* means 'roofed lizard'. This name was given because scientists in the 19th century thought that the plates lay flat along the back, like tiles on a roof. We now know that this was not true and that they stood upright. The proper name for these plates is scutes but most people still use the word plates.

At the start, scientists had no idea what this new mystery animal would have looked like and how it would have behaved. The only thing they could think was that it must have looked like and

acted like a super-sized turtle, because the idea of dinosaurs was still very new. Now, we obviously know a lot more about dinosaurs and can tell a lot more about the life of cool characters such as *Stegosaurus*.

So You Think You Know About Dinosaurs?

What is one of the most important parts of the skeleton to help us tell whether we're looking at a dinosaur or something else?

•

Which of these animals was not a dinosaur? *Pterosaurus? Dimetrodon? Gigantspinosaurus?*

•

When did *Dimetrodon* live?

•

What are the two species of *Stegosaurus* we can be sure of?

•

What was special about *Gigantspinosaurus?*

All the answers are in the text and at the back of the book.

CHAPTER 3

Dinosaur Discoveries

WHEN AND WHERE

WHEN AND WHERE

The times the dinosaurs were around can be split into three main chunks of time (what we call 'periods'). These are the **Triassic period**, the **Jurassic period** and the **Cretaceous period**. *Stegosaurus* lived towards the end of the Jurassic. At the end of the Triassic, there was a huge extinction, which the dinosaurs luckily survived (unlike the one at the end of the Cretaceous). This meant that throughout the Jurassic, there was a lot of space for new species to evolve, and within a few million years there were loads of dinosaurs of all shapes and sizes.

One group that did well was the Jurassic armoured dinosaurs like *Stegosaurus* and its relatives. There were many different armoured dinosaurs, but *Stegosaurus* is one of the best known from this time. The Jurassic lasted for 56.3 million years, from 201.3 million years ago to the beginning of the Cretaceous, 145 million years ago. *Stegosaurus* lived during the Late Jurassic, between 155 million and 150 million years ago.

Where was *Stegosaurus* found?
During the early time of the dinosaurs, most of the land on Earth formed a huge supercontinent called

THE WORLD IN THE LATE JURASSIC PERIOD

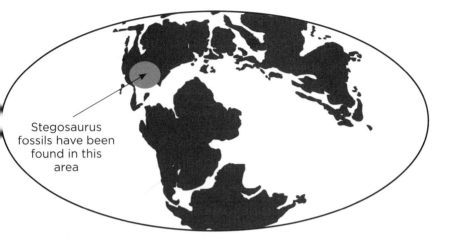

Stegosaurus fossils have been found in this area

Pangaea but during the Jurassic, this one big lump of land began to split into two major landmasses, Gondwana in the south and Laurasia to the north. *Stegosaurus* fossils are now found in certain places in the western United States of America, such as Colorado, Wyoming and Utah.

Their fossils are also found the other side of the Atlantic Ocean, in Portugal. They obviously didn't fly there and they didn't swim. . . they walked there. This happened millions of years ago, when the two areas were joined up, before the Laurasia broke up and started to make the continents such as North America and Europe that we recognise today.

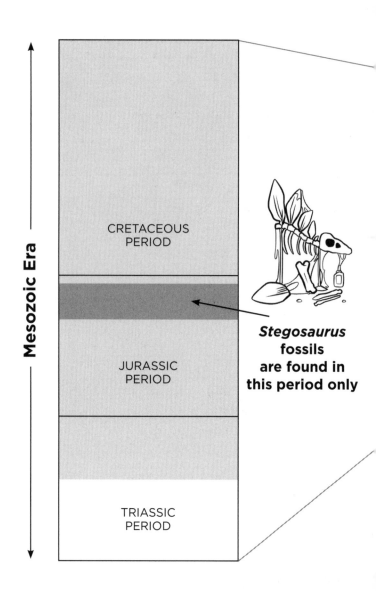

Mesozoic Era

CRETACEOUS
PERIOD

JURASSIC
PERIOD

TRIASSIC
PERIOD

Stegosaurus
**fossils
are found in
this period only**

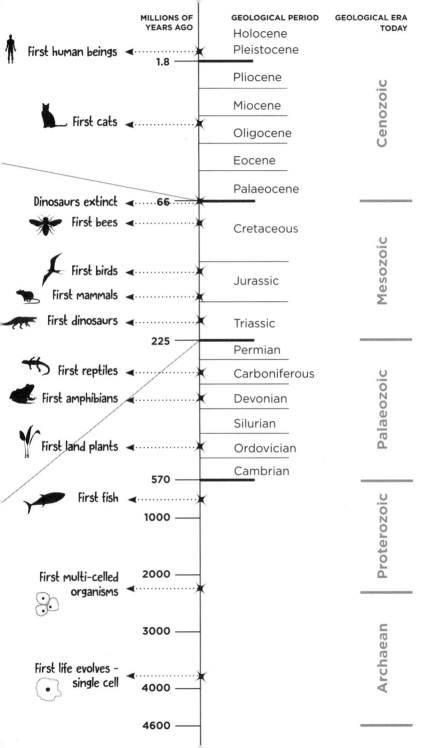

	MILLIONS OF YEARS AGO	GEOLOGICAL PERIOD	GEOLOGICAL ERA TODAY
First human beings	1.8	Holocene / Pleistocene	Cenozoic
First cats		Pliocene / Miocene / Oligocene / Eocene	
Dinosaurs extinct	66	Palaeocene	
First bees		Cretaceous	Mesozoic
First birds		Jurassic	
First mammals			
First dinosaurs	225	Triassic	
First reptiles		Permian / Carboniferous	Palaeozoic
First amphibians		Devonian	
First land plants		Silurian / Ordovician	
	570	Cambrian	
First fish	1000		Proterozoic
First multi-celled organisms	2000		
	3000		
First life evolves – single cell	4000		Archaean
	4600		

Why did *Stegosaurus* have plates and spines?

So many people work with dinosaurs –
from amateur collectors to world-famous scientists.
Some go looking for fossils in the ground, others study
them in laboratories and some recreate them
as incredible pieces of artwork.

DR SUSIE MAIDMENT

Palaeontologist

Natural History Museum, London (UK)

Dr Susie Maidment works at the Natural History Museum and is one of the top experts in the world on *Stegosaurus* and its close relatives. She also looks at what rock sediment at fossil sites can tell us and how they change over time and she was part of the team that discovered blood cells in a 75 million-year-old dinosaur bone. We asked her, 'Why did *Stegosaurus* have plates and spines?'

'Although *Stegosaurus* is one of the most easily recognisable dinosaurs, its fossils are surprisingly rare, and there's lots we still don't know about how it lived. It had two rows of plates that run from its neck to the tail, and at the end of its tail were four spikes. But what was *Stegosaurus* doing with those plates and spikes? What was their function? The spikes are fairly fearsome, and it seems most likely that *Stegosaurus* used them as a weapon: research has shown that it could swing its tail from side to side and impart a bone-crunching swipe on any predator brave enough to attack it. There is even a vertebra – a bone from the back – of *Allosaurus*, which has a hole in it that is thought to have been made by a *Stegosaurus* tail spike!

But what about the plates? What was their function? Researchers have come up with a number of ideas about what *Stegosaurus* might have used them for. The first is for defence: the plates could have protected the animal from a predator's bite. Another idea is that they were used for thermoregulation. This means that they helped the animal control its body temperature. Unlike us and other mammals, dinosaurs like *Stegosaurus* were probably cold-blooded. This means that they couldn't control their body temperature like mammals do, by sweating or panting to cool down. *Stegosaurus* was quite big, around 3m in length, and it weighed around 2 tonnes. A major problem for dinosaurs like *Stegosaurus* was that once they had warmed up, they needed to lose the body heat that they generated from walking about, digesting their food, and all of the other processes that go on in the body.

Some researchers have suggested that *Stegosaurus* used its plates like heat radiators: once the blood was too warm in the body, it could be pumped up and passed into the plates, and that blood would cool down as it came close to the surface of the skin on the plates.

Another idea for the function of *Stegosaurus* plates is display. Perhaps it was using them to look scary and deter predators from attacking it, like the stripy

48

colouring on a wasp. Or maybe it was using them for identification, to recognise members of the same species and make sure it was hanging out with the right group.

There were lots of different types of stegosaur from all over the world. *Stegosaurus* only lived in the USA, but there were two stegosaurs from the UK, *Dacentrurus* and *Loricatosaurus*. There were also quite a few different types from China.

In my research, I have noticed that all the different types of stegosaur have differently shaped plates and spikes. In China, it looks as though there were different types of stegosaur living alongside each other in the same environments. I think this means that stegosaur plates evolved for display, and that they were using them to make sure they were hanging out and mating with the right species. But the plates of the actual *Stegosaurus* are unique because they are so large and flat, and I suspect that *Stegosaurus* may also have been using its plates to help it cool down.

It's quite difficult to test these ideas, but right now, some palaeontologists are using engineering techniques that are usually used to improve performance in F1 racing cars and understand how air moves over aeroplane wings to see if *Stegosaurus* could have used its plates as heat radiators.

CHAPTER 4

Delve into a Dinosaur

ANATOMY OF *STEGOSAURUS*

THE BONES

The skeleton of any animal tells us a lot about how that animal moved, ate and behaved. The *Stegosaurus* skeleton is a brilliant example and tells us loads and loads about the living animal. Nothing had a skeleton like *Stegosaurus.*

THE SKULL

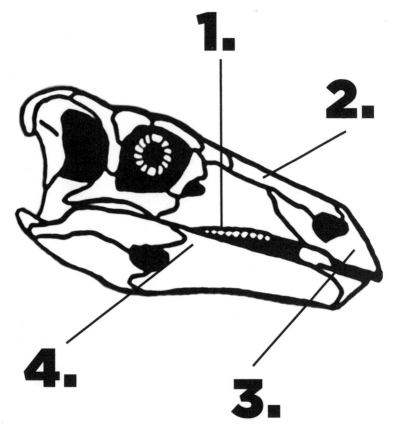

1. Many herbivorous dinosaurs with beaks (such as *Triceratops* and *Edmontosaurus*) had strong jaws and teeth that were perfectly shaped for grinding food. Instead, *Stegosaurus* teeth were small, rounded and looked like little pegs. Some scientists think it had cheeks and could chew its food but I'm not sure I agree with this – if it could only move its jaws up and down, that would make chewing very hard. Try eating your breakfast with just 'up and down' chews. Then try allowing your jaws to go side to side and see which is easier.

2. Most dinosaurs had a hole on either side of the skull, between the eye and nose, just in front of the eye, called the antorbital fenestra (*ann tor-bit-al fen ess-tra*), meaning 'window in front of the eye'. But the *Stegosaurus* did not have an antorbital fenestra.

3. The skull of *Stegosaurus* was long and narrow, with a pointed snout.

4. You can open and close your jaws and wiggle them from side to side, but some dinosaurs, such as *Triceratops* could only move its jaws up and down. *Stegosaurus* was the same and scientists think it used its jaws like a pair of scissors, cutting and snipping food.

These skulls are from three different herbivore dinosaurs:

a) *Stegosaurus*

b) *Erlikosaurus*

c) *Plateosaurus*

They were all used in some research to see how strong the bite of a *Stegosaurus* was. The skulls look similar, but the bones show us the dinosaurs fed differently. *Stegosaurus* did not have the antorbital fenestra (a hole between the eye socket and nostril), so its skull was stronger and it had a more powerful bite than many other prehistoric herbivores. It makes sense if you think about it – holes in something don't make it stronger. Its bite force was probably the same as a cow's and only half as strong as a human's.

Another thing scientists are unsure about is if *Stegosaurus* had a beak at the end of its mouth. There were no front teeth and the end of the skull was narrow, meaning a beak would have been possible. If there was a beak there, it would have been made from keratin (the same material that makes up your hair and finger nails) and may have looked a bit like the beak of a turtle. The truth is that scientists do not totally understand how *Stegosaurus* ate as yet.

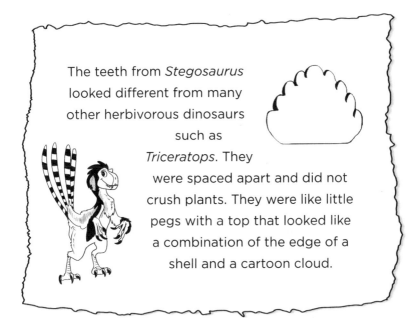

The teeth from *Stegosaurus* looked different from many other herbivorous dinosaurs such as *Triceratops*. They were spaced apart and did not crush plants. They were like little pegs with a top that looked like a combination of the edge of a shell and a cartoon cloud.

THE SKELETON

1.

There were between 17 and 22 plates that ran from the neck to the end of the tail.

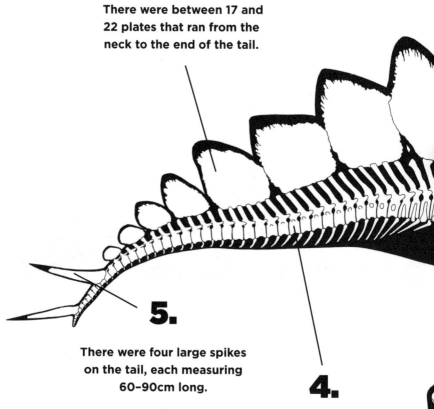

5.

There were four large spikes on the tail, each measuring 60–90cm long.

1m

4.

Scientists discovered that the tendons in the tail were stetchy and loose, making it more flexible than in many other dinosaurs.

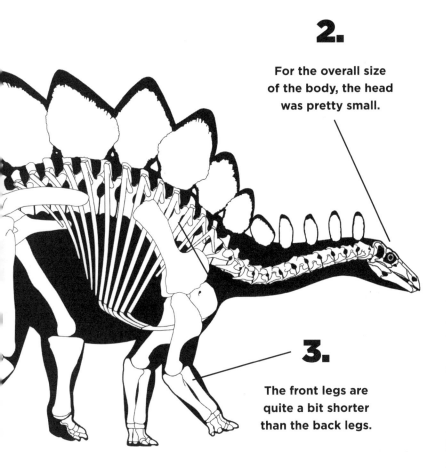

2.

For the overall size of the body, the head was pretty small.

3.

The front legs are quite a bit shorter than the back legs.

1. There
were between 17
and 22 plates that
ran from the neck
to the end of the tail.

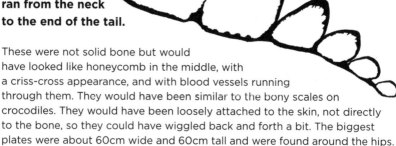

These were not solid bone but would
have looked like honeycomb in the middle, with
a criss-cross appearance, and with blood vessels running
through them. They would have been similar to the bony scales on
crocodiles. They would have been loosely attached to the skin, not directly
to the bone, so they could have wiggled back and forth a bit. The biggest
plates were about 60cm wide and 60cm tall and were found around the hips.

2. For the overall size of the body, the head was pretty small.

The body lengths of *Stegosaurus* and *Triceratops* were similar but the
Stegosaurus head was much, much smaller than that of its horned relative.

3. The front legs are quite a bit shorter
than the back legs.

The shape of the body looked weird, with the tail
up and the head low. This is because the front legs
are quite a bit shorter than the back legs. The head
was probably about 1m from the ground. This was
both bad and good. It was bad because it meant
that *Stegosaurus* would have been a very slow
dinosaur and running would have been difficult, if
not impossible. With short front legs and long back
legs, it would have become all tangled up if it had
tried to run and it may have fallen over. The good
thing was that because the head was low, it was
perfect for eating vegetation close to the
ground. *Stegosaurus* didn't need to waste
time bending down to eat – it was always
ready for food.

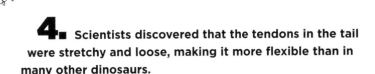

4. ■ **Scientists discovered that the tendons in the tail were stretchy and loose, making it more flexible than in many other dinosaurs.**

If the spikes were used for fighting, then they would have been rubbish weapons if the tail was stiff. It would have been better if the tail was flexible. Scientists have discovered that the tendons (the stretchy cords attaching muscles to bones) in the tail were stretchy and loose, making the *Stegosaurus* tail more flexible than in many other dinosaurs, and perfect for swinging the four deadly spikes at the end.

5. ■ **There were four large spikes on the tail. Each measured 60–90cm long.**

When trying to decide if they were used for display or for fighting, scientists found that about 10 per cent of *Stegosaurus* fossils had damaged tail spikes, meaning they were being used to hit things, either other stegosaurs or predators. The spikes came out of the tail in a horizontal position, which means they could have been slashed from side to side.

THE BODY

4.

The *Stegosaurus* stomach and gut was very large, meaning it could digest lots of tough plants.

3.

If you compare the size of its brain to the total body size, it had one of the smallest brains of any dinosaur.

2.

Stegosaurus may have had a beak like a parrot or turtle, made from keratin.

1.

Having a head close to the ground meant *Stegosaurus* was perfectly adapted for eating low-growing vegetation.

7.

Each front foot had five toes but only the inner two toes had a hoof that was blunt.

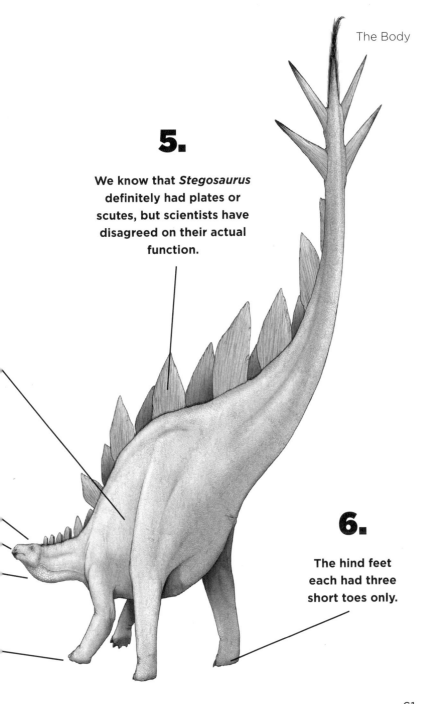

5.

We know that *Stegosaurus* definitely had plates or scutes, but scientists have disagreed on their actual function.

6.

The hind feet each had three short toes only.

1. The low position of the *Stegosaurus* head was not a mistake. Giraffes and sauropods have heads high off the ground so they can eat from trees and other tall plants. Having a head close to the ground meant *Stegosaurus* was perfectly adapted for eating low-growing vegetation, such as ferns, moss, cycads and even some fruits.

2. Although we are not yet certain, *Stegosaurus* may have had a beak like a parrot or turtle, made from keratin. To see if this was likely or not, scientists have done computer experiments to estimate the effect a beak would have made on the stress in the skull. The experiments showed that when a beak was added to a CGI *Stegosaurus*, the overall stress to the skull did not change. When scientists looked at the stress in the snout and the lower jaw, it was actually lower when a beak was added. This doesn't mean that *Stegosaurus* had a beak, it just means that if it did then it might have had some benefits.

3. It's never nice to say something is stupid but we've been saying that about *Stegosaurus* for years and years. If you compare the size of its brain to the total body size, it had one of the smallest brains of any dinosaur. We originally thought the brain was about the size and shape of a walnut or conker, but it now seems as though it looked more like a bent sausage. At one point, scientists thought *Stegosaurus* had such a small brain (and must have been so stupid) that it needed an 'extra brain'. They thought this second brain would have sat in a special little bony pocket, somewhere near the hips. Thankfully, we now no longer think that *Stegosaurus* had a spare brain in its bum.

4. It looks as though the jaws could only move up and down like a pair of scissors, which means that food could not be chewed up much. If you don't chew your food well, then it's harder to digest when it gets to your stomach and intestines. It takes a lot longer. One way to overcome this is to have really big guts. Gorillas and hippos are the same. They have large guts which allow the hard-to-digest plant material enough time and space to digest properly. The *Stegosaurus* stomach and gut was very large, meaning it could digest lots of tough plants. If you think about gorillas, elephants and even cows, they all have big guts to help them break down lots of tough vegetation.

5. We know that *Stegosaurus* definitely had plates or scutes, but scientists have disagreed on their actual function. Were they armour, used to impress mates or warn off predators or did they play a part in keeping the dinosaur warm or cool as needed? Have a look at Ask an Expert on pages 45–50 to find out more about this.

6. The hind feet each had three short toes only.

7. Each front foot had five toes but only the inner two toes had a hoof that was blunt.

Just after they were discovered, scientists thought that *Stegosaurus* looked very different to the way we now depict them. We used to think some had eight vertical tail spikes. We now know they had four tail spikes which stuck out horizontally. Some scientists thought the tail spikes sat on the wrists and were used to fight when the animals stood on its back legs. We also used to think that the mighty *Stegosaurus* was fat and slow and that its head and tail both hung close to the ground, but we know that they didn't look as though they were really

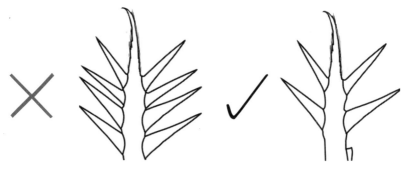

sleepy all the time. The biggest difference, though, is that it used to be thought the plates sat on the back and hung over the side. Now everyone knows that the most obvious things about a *Stegosaurus* were that the big plates running down its back stood upright.

The *Stegosaurus* tail weapons have two names. The first is 'tail spikes' and the second is 'thagomizers' (*thaggo mize-erzz*). This name came from a cartoon joke (1982). The artist drew a bunch of cavemen who were upset because their friend Thag had been killed by a *Stegosaurus*. They said because a spike killed him, it should be called a Thagomizer. First of

all, humans (even early ones) never lived at the same time as dinosaurs and secondly, some scientists say 'thagomizers' and some prefer 'tail spikes'. Which name do you use?

CHAPTER 5

Dinosaur Domains

HABITATS AND ECOSYSTEMS

HABITATS AND ECOSYSTEMS

Looking at the anatomy of the *Stegosaurus*, with its short neck, head held low and teeth that were not able to chew or break down tough vegetation, scientists believe that it ate lots of different plants that grew close to the ground.

It probably ate a range of bushes and trees, as well as ferns, conifers, mosses, horsetails, cycads and fruits. Although we are not certain yet, some scientists believe that *Stegosaurus* could stand on its back legs to reach higher up and get more food.

Because we're not yet 100 per cent sure that *Stegosaurus* could stand up on its back legs, we don't really know exactly what it ate. If it only stood on all four legs, then it could eat things from the ground to maybe

one metre up, but if it was able to stand up on its back legs, then everything from the ground up to maybe six metres high was available. This would have made a big difference to how it fed, giving it more types of food. And it would not have had to walk so far for a meal each time. One day we'll know for sure. Either way,

Stegosaurus was probably really important in spreading cycad seeds through the habitat, tucked away in their very own little package of ready-made 'fertiliser'. Think about it . . .

There have been some big extinction events throughout prehistory, such as at the end of the Triassic, when 80 per cent of species on Earth died, and famously at the end of the Cretaceous, when the giant asteroid struck and led to the extinction of more than 75 per cent of species. But other species died out for different reasons. Why, for example, did *Stegosaurus* suddenly die out in the Early Cretaceous? Lots of other dinosaurs happily lived on while they died out. Flowers! Flowers killed *Stegosaurus*. The types of plants started to change around the start of the Cretaceous and flowering plants evolved. At the same time, plants like cycads started to die out. *Stegosaurus* had not evolved to eat the new plants and would have found it harder and harder to find food. Over time, as these new flowering plants started to take over, *Stegosaurus* would have found it harder and harder to find food. Eventually, with less food and new species of dinosaurs that could eat a wider range of plants, poor old *Stegosaurus* would have slowly slipped into the history books.

When it was alive, *Stegosaurus* lived in a habitat with lots of rivers, lakes, wetlands and sand dunes. The whole area regularly flooded, which meant it was green and lush, but dry in other seasons. There were only a few trees around like monkey-puzzle trees, but mostly there were lots of ferns, cycads, conifers, horsetails, mosses, algae and fungi.

There were lots of other dinosaurs living in the same place at the same time as *Stegosaurus*. Sauropods were common in the area but there were also some serious predators around, and *Allosaurus* was probably the main predator of most animals then. Which of the following names do you recognise?

Stegosaurus fossils are often found at the same sites as *Allosaurus, Apatosaurus, Camarasaurus*, and *Diplodocus*.

Sauropods:

Apatosaurus*

Diplodocus*

Brachiosaurus*

Camarasaurus

Barosaurus

Theropods:

Ceratosaurus*

Allosaurus*

Torvosaurus

Coelurus

Ornithischians:

Camptosaurus

Dryosaurus

Drinker

So You Think You Know About Dinosaurs?

When did *Stegosaurus* live?

•

How many tail spikes did
Stegosaurus have?

•

What's another name for
Stegosaurus' tail spikes?

•

How many toes did *Stegosaurus*
have on its hind feet?

•

Why did *Stegosaurus*
become extinct?

All the answers are in the text
and at the back of the book.

So What Sounds Did Dinosaurs Make?

We all know dinosaurs have a fearsome, earth-shaking roar – right? Or did they? For the answer to this question, I knew exactly who to chat to – my colleague Dr Darren Naish who is a palaeontologist and science writer based in the UK. His reply might surprise you.

Let's set the scene: Imagine two dinosaurs fighting for survival, slashing their tails at each other and baring teeth and claws. We understand so much about the science behind dinosaurs now that this fight is easier to picture, but try to imagine what noises they made. Did they roar? Did they hiss? Or were they silent? Like anything in science, we need to look at the evidence.

'Why do we think dinosaurs growled, bellowed or roared? It's a popular idea and has been depicted time and again in movies and TV shows. The notion that dinosaurs roared is generally favoured for dramatic reasons (we all love the idea of a terrifying *T. rex* roar), but what does science actually tell us about the noise-making abilities of these animals?

Our knowledge of dinosaur anatomy – combined with what we know about animals alive today – makes it likely that extinct dinosaurs did use sound in communication. The head crests of duckbilled hadrosaurs, the gigantic noses of horned dinosaurs and the long, air-filled neck skeletons of sauropods all look as if they were used in amplifying or resonating calls made in the throat or chest and broadcast to the outside world via the snout or mouth. If you look at animals alive today that are closely related to dinosaurs (like crocodiles and birds) all use sound for courtship, battle and other forms of communication.

However, crocodylians and birds use different organs to generate these sounds. Crocodylians use the larynx *(la-rinks)* in the throat, while birds use the  syrinx *(siir-rinks)* in the chest. Did dinosaurs have one, both or neither of these organs? At the moment we're not sure, though it appears likely that some non-bird dinosaurs had a larynx and it's *possible* that some bird-like dinosaurs had a syrinx. If extinct dinosaurs did have

 either of these structures, the noises they made would probably have been hisses or low, rumbling sounds made with a closed mouth.

It is at least possible that all kinds of noises were present across dinosaurs, such as squawking and cooing, but at the moment, there is no clear support for it and as scientists, we always need to look at the evidence in front of us.

But what about the open-mouth, lion-like roaring of Hollywood dinosaurs? Well, it doesn't look at all likely as a possibility, so meeting a *Tyrannosaurus rex* in the street would still have been scary but it almost definitely wouldn't have roared at you!'

Some exciting new fossils have been recently found and scientists are looking into what sounds they may have made. Perhaps some of the predatory dinosaurs cooed a bit like a pigeon or even honked like a goose. The truth is that we don't know yet, but watch this space, as we may soon know exactly how the dinosaurs sounded.

CHAPTER 6

Dodging Dinosaurs

EVOLUTIONARY ARMS RACE

EVOLUTIONARY ARMS RACE

Lots of things drive evolution forward, making a species change over time. It could be the particular habitat (such as a cold environment makes polar bears have very small ears), or feeding techniques (just think about giraffes), but it might be down to competition between predators and prey. The term for this is an evolutionary arms race, where, as the predator species evolves in a way to increase its chances of catching and eating the prey, the prey species also evolves to reduce the chances of ending up as lunch. Then the predator evolves to increase its chances again and so does the prey, and so on and so on. It never ends and both species are trying to do what is best for them.

Many 'prey' animals have a bunch of adaptations that look confusing. They can either be used for their own species (either to find a mate or to scare off a competitor) or against predators. If you think about horns on animals like white rhinos and African buffalos, there is often a little of both. The same adaptations can be used for display and as weapons but with extinct animals such as dinosaurs we don't have much evidence for behaviour. As every good scientist does, you should always be asking yourself 'Where's the proof, where's the evidence?' This battle is based on actual fossil evidence, where scientists have pieced together what the relationship between *Stegosaurus* and its main predator, *Allosaurus*, might have been like.

THE BATTLE

It's the start of the rainy season, 152 million years ago. It's early morning and the air is still cool. There is a thick mist. It's hard to see very far but noises, like the low rumbles of a *Stegosaurus* herd eating a patch of horsetails, carry through the mist. Their huge tummies rumble as they crunch and eat. The mist is clearing slightly but it's still hard to see.

One big male *Stegosaurus* is feeding alone, away from the others, near a pile of towering boulders. His huge plates sway lazily on his back and his long, deadly tail spikes are hidden in the bushes as he feeds. As the mist lifts, he raises his head and spots a female *Allosaurus* close by. She has been stalking the *Stegosaurus* for an hour under cover of the patchy mist. Now she moves closer, lowers her head and opens her vast mouth to reveal big, sharp teeth. The *Stegosaurus* responds by lifting his head and bellowing, a deep, low rumble from within. His tail lifts and swings in a long, dangerous display, the spikes tearing through the bushes.

Other adult animals from the *Stegosaurus* herd circle their young to protect them from a possible attack. The big male shows the *Allosaurus* the side of his body as a threat. The plates have flushed with blood and their horny coverings have changed colour, showing thick stripy zig-zags as a serious warning. He turns his tail towards the attacking *Allosaurus* and waves it to and fro with powerful swipes, the 60cm spikes slashing the air loudly. The *Allosaurus* tries to get close to the vulnerable head and side of the *Stegosaurus*, but he keeps turning and turning, making sure his tail stops the predator. One accurate hit and the *Allosaurus* will be killed.

The huge *Stegosaurus* weighs over 7 tonnes and moves slowly but the *Allosaurus* weighs just over 1.5 tonnes and is much faster. She is not tired easily and is able to keep moving. As she keeps circling the *Stegosaurus*, she suddenly jumps onto his side and bites hard into one of the plates. The *Allosaurus* clings onto the back of the *Stegosaurus*, snapping more plates with her teeth. Her claws dig into the skin of his side, the *Stegosaurus* panics and hurls himself up, rearing onto his hind legs.

It is dangerous for the *Stegosaurus* to land heavily and it rarely stands on its hind legs, so it comes as a big surprise to the *Allosaurus* when she is suddenly six metres up in the air. Her grip is broken and she falls and lands awkwardly on the ground. The *Stegosaurus* moves quickly and lashes his tail towards the predator. One tail spike strikes her leg, damaging muscles and tendons. The *Stegosaurus* slams his tail against the injured *Allosaurus* and a deadly spike pierces her, burying itself deep in her tail, cutting through skin, muscle and bone. The huge *Stegosaurus* walks away, leaving the

STEGOSAURUS	
SPEED	2
AVERAGE WEIGHT (tonnes)	5
AGILITY	3
WEAPONS (teeth, horns)	8

injured predator lying on the ground, bleeding and barely alive.

This epic palaeo-battle was inspired by actual fossil evidence of *Stegosaurus-Allosaurus* encounters. A *Stegosaurus* back plate was found with a big U-shaped bite taken out

of it. When palaeontologists studied the tooth marks, they matched those of an *Allosaurus* perfectly. The best piece of evidence however that fights happened between *Stegosaurus* and *Allosaurus* came when palaeontologists found a tail vertebra from one of these deadly

ALLOSAURUS	
SPEED	7
AVERAGE WEIGHT (tonnes)	3
AGILITY	8
WEAPONS (teeth, horns)	5

predators with a nasty injury. The bone had a hole in it, where something long and sharp had pierced it with considerable force. When they looked, scientists found that the hole matched the size and shape of a *Stegosaurus* tail spike. Even cooler, they found that the bone had started to heal when the big *Allosaurus* died, meaning that after the fight in which it had been injured, the big predator survived, at least for a time.

Deadliest Dinosaurs?

In each *So You Think You Know About . . . Dinosaurs?* book you're able to read about a battle between different dinosaurs, battles in which predators and prey fight, angry herbivores compete with each other or predators attack one another. Each time, evidence from real fossil finds is used to recreate an epic palaeo-battle.

Here though, you can find out which really was the deadliest dinosaur by imagining them all fighting against each other. Fill in the chart on the next page by deciding which dinosaur would win in a fight. Don't just pick the biggest or the one with the sharpest teeth. Think about their weapons and defences. Think about whether the dinosaur was an adult or juvenile, or whether it was male or female. Each of these

Dodging Dinosaurs

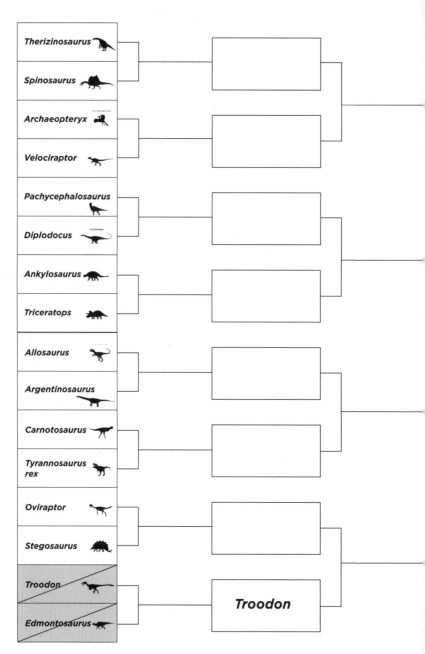

Therizinosaurus

Spinosaurus

Archaeopteryx

Velociraptor

Pachycephalosaurus

Diplodocus

Ankylosaurus

Triceratops

Allosaurus

Argentinosaurus

Carnotosaurus

Tyrannosaurus rex

Oviraptor

Stegosaurus

Troodon

Edmontosaurus

Troodon

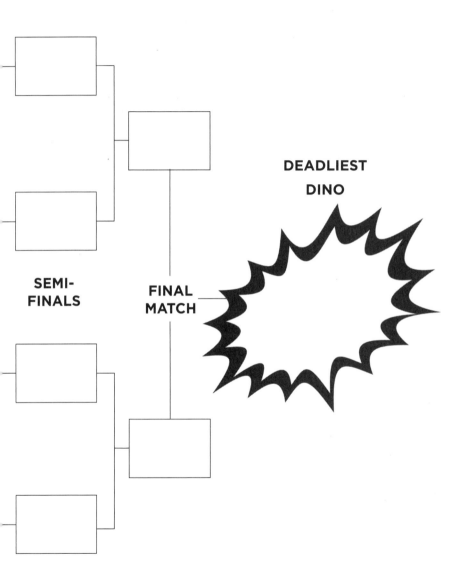

**SEMI-
FINALS**

**FINAL
MATCH**

**DEADLIEST
DINO**

things makes a difference. In the first fight, where an *Edmontosaurus* and a *Troodon* do battle, the *Troodon* wins, because the fight happens at night.

The *Troodon* had the biggest brain of any dinosaur (for its body size) and also some of the biggest eyes. In my mind, this imaginary fight takes place at night. The *Edmontosaurus* was young and couldn't see the predator. The *Troodon* had sharp teeth and claws and won the fight when it managed to bite the *Edmontosaurus* on the throat. Have fun in discovering which you think really was the most deadly dinosaur.

Fossil Finder

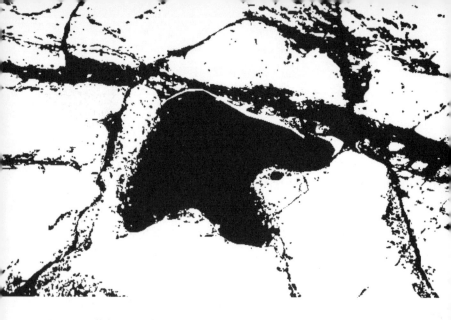

As you'll know from my other *So You Think You Know About . . . Dinosaurs?* titles, fossils come in all shapes and sizes and you can have great fun collecting them. Just make sure it's safe to do so and you collect in an area that won't damage the environment. Some fossils you can pick up and hold, such as bones, teeth and ammonites but there are other types of fossils too. Trace fossils are a really important type of fossil but usually you can't just pick them up. Trace fossils are a record not only of bones, skin and feathers but of behaviours. They can tell us how a dinosaur walked or ran, whether it lived on its own or in groups and how it behaved. Most often, trace fossils are footprints and burrows but can also include coprolites (fossilised poos). Understanding the behaviour of an animal that died more than 66 million years ago may seem impossible, but trace

fossils can help us understand more about
dinosaur behaviour.

So how do you study them? Imagine a
Tyrannosaurus rex footprint in a fossilised streambed
in Montana or the print of a beautiful new species
of ammonite in a huge rock on the Jurassic Coast.
You should not try and take them with you (unless
you are a professional palaeontologist) and a
photograph won't always show the detail well.
Scientists now have access to high-tech lasers,
which can be fired at the trace fossil to
make a CGI copy. But before we had fancy
lasers, scientists took casts of the fossils
and studied them. Here's how to take a cast of a trace
fossil, so that you can keep a permanent record.

How to make a fossil cast
You will need some plaster of paris (which you can get
from most DIY and craft shops), water, a shiny strip of
paper or card, some paper clips and some modelling
clay like plasticine. Then you'll need to find a trace
fossil that you can take your cast from. If you can't find
a fossil of an ammonite or *Iguanodon* lying around,
then try making a cast of your own footprints on the
beach or in some damp soil.

When you have found your fossil, first make a loop with the shiny card or paper and secure it in a circle with the paper clips. The circle needs to be bigger than the fossil, so that the fossil fits inside. If there are gaps between the paper circle and the rock, make a circle of clay around the fossil and then push the paper circle into the clay so that the mixture doesn't escape. Now mix the Plaster of Paris and water in a bowl. You will need a spoon or stick to mix it and to remove any lumps. There is no magic recipe here – you will become an expert after you have done this a few times – but the mixture should be not too runny or too thick.

If the mixture is too thin, the cast will take ages to set and will break easily. If it is too thick, then it will set too quickly and won't record the details on the fossil. The mixture should be as thick as custard or thick cream.

Make sure the fossil is clean either by blowing or brushing away any dirt. Once it is clean and you have the perfect mixture, slowly pour it on the trace fossil or into the footprint. Pour the mixture into the fossil directly so that every bit is covered. The mixture should be at least 2cm thick when you pour it into the paper circle, so that it doesn't break easily when it dries. The plaster will take about ten minutes to dry properly.

BE SAFE

You may want to take a cast of your hand but it can be very dangerous to put your hand in plaster mixture for a long time. The plaster becomes very, very hot and can cause burns. It's okay to get it on your fingers and hands when mixing it but do not place your hands *in* the mixture *when* it's drying. If you want to mould your hands, there is special mixture from craft shops.

After ten minutes, tap on the surface of the mixture. It should be solid now. If you can press your finger into it, it's not quite ready yet. When you're sure it's dry, gently lift the whole cast from the fossil or footprint and remove the paper circle. Remember that the cast you have made is a 'reverse print' of the trace fossil. Clean your fossil cast with a brush, to remove any sand or dirt. If you really want to, you can use some paint to highlight parts of the cast (I prefer to just leave it).

All trace fossils tell us something about the animal that created it. What do these prints tell you about these dinosaurs?

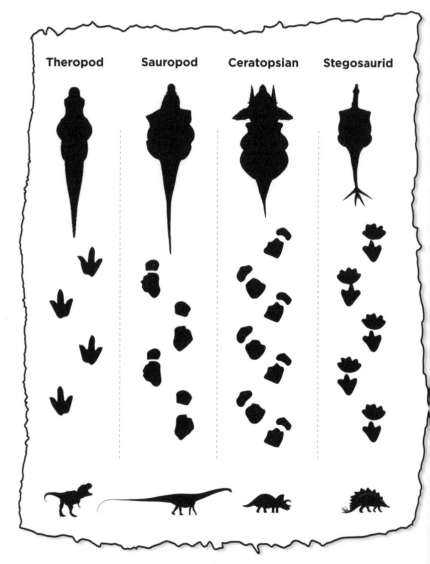

Theropod	Sauropod	Ceratopsian	Stegosaurid

Because you are a young scientist, you need to record all the details you can. On the back of the cast, use a pencil to write the date and location where you made the cast and if you can, what species the cast is from.

You could even have fun and use some big dinosaur toys to make prints in sand or mud and then take your own casts.

Quiz Answers

p 38

What is one of the most important parts of the skeleton to help us tell whether we're looking at a dinosaur or something else?

The skull.

Which of these animals was not a dinosaur? *Pterosaurus? Dimetrodon? Gigantspinosaurus?*

Pterosaurus and *Dimetrodon*.

When did *Dimetrodon* live?

270 million years ago in the Permian.

What are the two species of *Stegosaurus* we can be sure of?

Stegosaurus ungulatus and *Stegosaurus stenops*.

What was special about *Gigantspinosaurus*?

Two massive shoulder spines.

p 72

When did *Stegosaurus* live?
Late Jurassic, 155–150 million years ago.

How many tail spikes did *Stegosaurus* have?
Four.

What's another name for *Stegosaurus's* tail spikes?
Thagomizer.

How many toes did *Stegosaurus* have on its hind feet?
Three short toes.

Why did *Stegosaurus* become extinct?
Cycads and the other plants it ate died out
and it became hard to find food. It did not evolve.

How many did you get?

Glossary

Jog your memory here

Ammonites These were squid-like animals that had rounded, flattened shells and lived in the ocean. They were alive between 400 million and 66 million years ago. Their shells are commonly found on rocky shores where other Jurassic and Cretaceous fossils are discovered.

Cretaceous A geological period in the history of the Earth.

Cycad A group of plants with a very long fossil record. They were more common in prehistoric times. They usually had a thick woody trunk and a 'crown' of large, stiff, evergreen leaves. Cycads can range from a few centimetres to several metres high. Some live up to 1,000 years.

Diapsid Means 'two arches'. This group includes crocodiles, lizards, snakes, turtles and dinosaurs.

Ecosystem The network (or community) of species all interacting in one particular environment.

Ectotherm An animal that needs the outside environment to make heat within its body. Good examples of ectotherms are the reptiles. Another term often used instead of ectotherm is 'cold-blooded' but this is not a good term because 'cold-blooded' animals still have 'warm' blood. The only difference is that their blood is warmed up by something in the environment, such as the sun, outside the body.

Endotherm An animal that is able to make heat within its own body. Good examples of endotherms are the mammals. Another phrase used instead of endotherm is 'warm-blooded' but look at the definition for 'ectotherm' – these animals have 'warm' blood too.

Femur The proper name for the thigh bone, in the upper leg. In many species, it is the largest bone in the body.

Fenestra The name given to a little hole in a bone. This does not include a hole made by an injury and does not cover every hole, but some are officially known as a fenestra. The word is French for 'window'.

Genus A level of classification in biology above the species. Each animal (including humans) has a scientific name made from two parts, the genus and the species. One good example is *Tyrannosaurus rex* – *Tyrannosaurus* is the genus and *rex* is the species.

Herbivore Any animal that relies on plants for its diet.

Jurassic A geological period in the history of the Earth.

Keratin Horny material found on lots of different animals. It is the material that makes up hair, finer nails and horns.

Mesotherm These are animals that are not quite endotherms and not quite ectotherms. Tuna, great white sharks and even echidnas are examples of mesotherms. Mesotherms cannot control their body temperature as well as a human or a dog can but they do not rely on the environment (for heating the body) in the same way that a reptile does. We still do not fully understand how mesotherms work.

Palaeontologist A scientist who uses fossils to help study and understand more. Palaeontologists can study lots of things, including dinosaurs, plants, mammals, insects and fish.

Pelvis The area of the hips. The group of bones in and around the hips is called the pelvis, even though it is made up from several bones fused together.

Synapsid Means 'fused arch' and includes mammals and some earlier groups. Synapsids have skulls with a hole behind each eye, which allows strong muscle attachments to the jaw.

Theropod One of the many dinosaurs that have two legs and are usually carnivorous. *Tyrannosaurus rex, Allosaurus, Spinosaurus* and *Velociraptor* are all theropods.

Triassic A geological period in the history of the Earth.

Visit

www.bengarrod.co.uk

for lots more about
dinosaurs

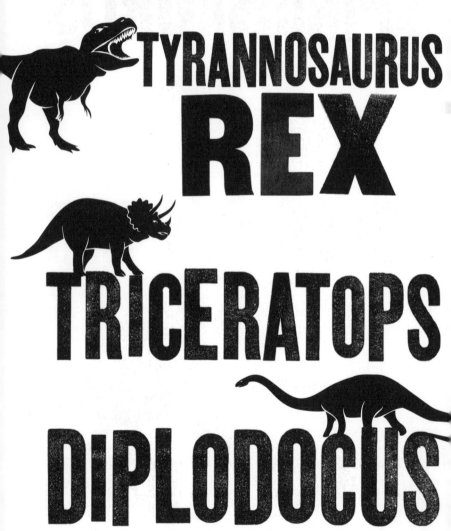
BEN GARROD
So You Think You Know About...?
TYRANNOSAURUS REX
TRICERATOPS
DIPLODOCUS

SPINOSAURUS

VELOCIRAPTOR

STEGOSAURUS

At Zephyr we are proud to publish books you can read and re-read time and time again because they tell a brilliant story and because they entertain you.

That's why we've launched the Zephyr Review Crew. We'd like to hear about the things you love in our books and what you think we could do better.

Join our review crew and be the first to read the very best new books. Members will receive exclusive author content and chances to win signed books. Just drop us a line at hello@headofzeus.com

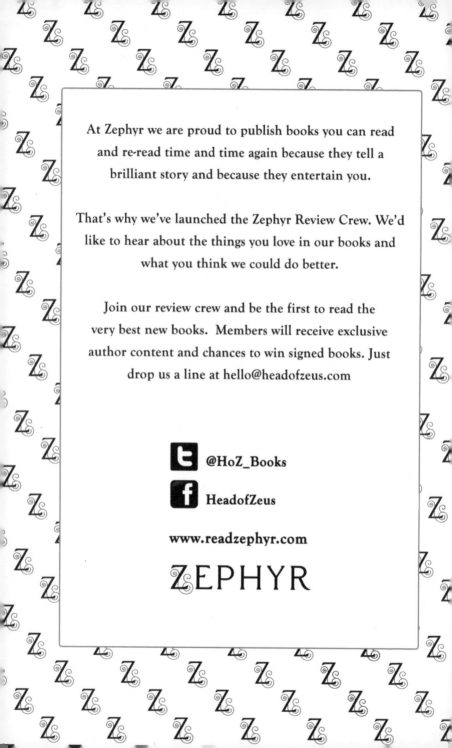 @HoZ_Books

HeadofZeus

www.readzephyr.com

ZEPHYR